Complicity

poems by

Steve Wilson

Finishing Line Press
Georgetown, Kentucky

Complicity

Copyright © 2023 by Steve Wilson
ISBN 979-8-88838-130-4 First Edition
All rights reserved under International and Pan-American Copyright Conventions. No part of this book may be reproduced in any manner whatsoever without written permission from the publisher, except in the case of brief quotations embodied in critical articles and reviews.

ACKNOWLEDGMENTS

A number of poems in this collection, some in earlier versions, appeared in the following journals and electronic publications:

Blue Unicorn
The Christian Century
Commonweal
High Plains Literary Review
Indolent Books' "Transition: Poems in the Afterglow"
Midwest Quarterly
New Rivers Press' "Poem-A-Day"
Precipitate
Poem
San Pedro River Review
TejasCovido
Texas Observer

Publisher: Leah Huete de Maines
Editor: Christen Kincaid
Cover Art: Dorothy T. Lawrenson
Author Photo: Nancy Wilson
Cover Design: Elizabeth Maines McCleavy

Order online: www.finishinglinepress.com
also available on amazon.com

Author inquiries and mail orders:
Finishing Line Press
PO Box 1626
Georgetown, Kentucky 40324
USA

Table of Contents

Of course I must have imagined it. The door	1
Your Injuries	2
The Dead Sea	3
Prayer Along the Road	4
A Summer	5
Badbye	6
Eighteen Analects for Late-Stage America	7
Driving Through the Dark	8
Late July Afternoon Beside Cuskinny Marsh	9
Triolet for Election 2020	10
If you aren't dead, why does your body thrum?	11
Against Isolation	12
Massage	13
Pandemic Haiku for April Mornings	14
Post-Election Haiku, 2020	15
Restrictions	16
Self-Rules During Isolation	17
A Transfixion	18
On Uncertainty	19
Unmoored Triolet	20
2020	21
For Maria de la Luz Valverde	22
Another Bridget	23
Goodbye	24
Moon and Planet—	25
New York Winter, 49	26
Caught Music	27
Kepler's Last Autumn	28
Part	29
Goodwife's Prayer, Autumn 1653	30
Snow	31
Along Rockfall	32
Blue Salvia in August	33
Climbing Rose	34
Poets in Romania	35
Winter and Midnights	36

I   Because

Of course I must have imagined it. The door

was unlocked, profoundly open. Outside,
of motion and colors a whirlwind (autumn's
first blusterings, you'll understand), as if
landscape on becoming were intent, were bent
        on revisions. Knives and forks, teaspoons,

settled in the kitchen drawer, gleamed
like teeth. A metal alignment, insistent.
Of metals, growling their precisions.
Down the blue hall, later, leaves browned
        with menace: the dining-room table

centered within my own gauzy memory.
Furniture, trudging. Or so I now recall.
Suggestions full of heft and solidities,
something unworded—stolid as wall-
        paper. A footfall. A polished balustrade.

I Because

Your Injuries

Old Stick-in-the-Eye,
have a sit. Time to

clear-cut. The wide fields
are choked with grass stalks
and transgressions, browned

from blight. Till the guilt.
Open furrows for

airing venom, wounds
nursed in the craw since
we were kids. Gut-punch

someone. Throw something
hard. We're flesh to be

marred—you and me—so
a whiter sun can
blur our hurts. The rib's

bare—to knife through; to
muss, or mend, with pain.

Because

The Dead Sea

    * even by this releasing the urge to move
outward into something else where I am

aware of myself at least * afloating
    some seconds * set upon * lounging

    in this selfsame body * wrapped up in water
sweetly as it circles about me its arms

or what are they * currents yes * coaxing * draws me
    into * for how long then are we one

    or two * until there is only a shadow within
a light * this is all I want to remember *

I BECAUSE

Prayer Along the Road

For the pain of God, I curse myself.
For the pain of God, I turn my face from the world.
For the pain of God, in dark hallways I stumble toward the stairs.
For the pain of God, nothing but the insistence of trees.

What is the voice of forgiveness? What is the gesture that shapes His name?

For the pain of God, I think and think of no one.
For the pain of God, even children will be lost, standing near the playground.
For the pain of God, your words contain only shapes and lies.
For the pain of God, what is this body but blackness?

What is the voice of forgiveness? What is the gesture that shapes His name?

For the pain of God, may a sword slice through my flesh.
For the pain of God, only blood and blood and blood.
For the pain of God, compassion is the weakness for escape.
For the pain of God, all others are like orphans in burned villages.

What is the voice of forgiveness? What is the gesture that shapes His name?
What is the gesture that shapes His name? What is the gesture?

For the pain of God, as a flooding river we wash over the streets.
For the pain of God, the end cannot come too soon. We urge it come, come.
For the pain of God, I turn my face from the world.
I turn my face from the world.
I turn my face from the world.

I BECAUSE

A Summer

Live oaks on a faint July breeze

loose their yellowed leaves.
From our homestead of American possibilities,
we sit and watch the unease everywhere

deepen—a brittle, brown foetor
like grass scorched by drought,
the lawn bare down to dirt—it settles now

into spaces beneath the door, within sidewalk cracks.
Listen: the brutal world unmasks itself;
all illusions burned soon to gray ash.

Citizens muscled into unmarked vans.

Because

Badbye

I wish you regrets sharp as knives.
Glaucoma, insecurities, gaping lesions
left by soul-eaters, plague seasons.
I wish you regrets sharp as knives.

Wander into a labyrinth of gray spiders.
Trip headfirst into limbo, surrounded by grackles,
swallowed by sinkholes. Gagged. Shackled.
I wish you regrets sharp as knives.

Dead mice in your mattress—little parcels
of hair and teeth. Anxiety hazes. Horseflies
troubling your lungs. Rusting skies.
I wish you regrets sharp as knives.

There is no velvet bed of forgiveness.
There is no harmonium. Only brittle birds
at the heart's center—black-feathered words.
I wish you regrets sharp as knives.

Because

Eighteen Analects for Late-Stage America

This highway mind, through which we compose our violet and smog.
Winter of brown dogs, winter of transgressions, winter of chasms.
Wind worries rages, unfurls disaffection.
Your fear in mine—the beach seared white as an August noon.
I don't trust. I won't.
Police muster behind repurposed tanks. Fifth Street: their battlefield, lined with discount shoe stores.
Scissortails arc over the suburbs, shadowed within live oaks.
Coming up: Trumps.
Astrology makes a strange comeback as pastels, daywear—identities fashioned for evading.
Mugging for selfies, rioters instagram their insurrection.
Along the despairing months of spring.
Covid falsehoods callous as bad teeth. The GOP's "Masks of the Reds' Death."
Anyplace USA implodes apace, its possibilities crowded with gray pigeons.
Nicholas Cage redeems himself. James Bond delays the inevitable.
The Black Panthers have a Hollywood moment.
Each of us a target.
Strive to be canceled. Stumble into anonymity.
Whose false flag?
Born beside freedom, children hurl rocks at apartment windows.

II THEREFORE

Driving Through the Dark

she just
wants to
go and go and go—

drive
all the way to china maybe
and meet

someone by a river
and then
we'll see

II Therefore

Late July Afternoon Beside Cuskinny Marsh
    —Ireland, 2019

Within the abbreviating
shadows, a dunnock—
by us vexed to flight,

      now chattering
      its myriad dissatisfactions—troubles

the hedgerows. Midday
crests bright above
the ash and gray sallow.

II Therefore

Triolet for Election 2020
—after Gary Snyder

See clear: gray oaks by gales snapped, torn
    at the sinews. Answer.
See clear. Gray oaks by gales snapped, torn
        to kindling—here's your fire-
        start for growth. Work to
see. Clear gray. Oaks by gales snapped, torn
    at the sinews. Answer.

II Therefore

If you aren't dead, why does your body thrum?

If you aren't dead, why does your body thrum
with lethargy while you slumber

beside the window? Why do you wear light
like a greatcoat against movement?
If you aren't a self suspended

between, how to explain the blank hours,
the gathered sparrows? If you indeed hold here

even now, whose hollows afternoons
reach tremulous to embrace you?
Through canyons aflood and unearthed

with ravenous distance, who,
ghost-minded, welcomes the chase?

II Therefore

Against Isolation

>Late afternoon,
at the backyard
feeders, a few

>early spring song-
birds gather and

>hurry—oaks to
woodpile, from fence

>to windowsill—
as if distance

>were a belief
traced with their wings,

>landscape some thought
motion now by
flight revealed.

Massage

In his crisp brown shirt and badge,
pistol at the ready on his hip,
the officer parsed a slaughter:
"He was having a very bad day."

The tiny rooms are shattered
by screams, by gunshots cascading
along the walls. A woman's head turns.
"He was having a very bad day."

Sitting in his car an hour before (steeling
or softening?), he paused and prayed—
heard answers that roiled the very air.
"He was having a very bad day."

Three spaces painted red by violence;
it deepens now against the failing light—
evening approaching, and eight dead.
"He was having a very bad day."

II Therefore

Pandemic Haiku for April Mornings

Asimmer, Spring blooms,
                sings its extravagant greens.

Bells call from shut schools.

II THEREFORE

Post-Election Haiku, 2020

autumn and its uncertainties—

                light, the threadbare clouds,
     fraying above the trees

II Therefore

Restrictions

                                Days splinter
    like storm-split oaks, shred

            into threads of
                  light, shadow,
  across the lawn. Soon,

        perhaps: open moments
    certain as distance, as unwound as
        the wide and deepening

    wilds beyond
                our isolations.

Self-Rules During Isolation

Sundays, un-
        congregate. Debride
surfaces and systems.
Tongue's done
        stumped, speaking

distances from,
        metrics for. Realignments
among joggers who
mile after mile urge
        themselves on. I have

a white room
        houses my unease. Who wants
(from afar, someone,
after all) to see
        such need breathing?

II Therefore

A Transfixion

                                        Spun among dark
                               isolations, dreams all

        roil and shadows: like reeds
            bent beside the river, or clouds

   blown landward
      before a hurricane. Silence

                             troubled within
                             fracturing light.

On Uncertainty

Everywhere the weave
between us loosens,
weakens. Threads fray. This

morning, before light,
old fears, familiars—
windows rattled by

sudden thunder, sounds
shaped within darkness—
brought an odd comfort.

Who knows what, in doubt,
may carry us through?

II Therefore

Unmoored Triolet

Unmoored, faith now failing, we shape
      angels from the ether.
Unmoored faith. Now, failing, we shape
        a path toward, a way past
        that need conceives—balm for
unmoored faith, now failing. We shape
      angels from the ether.

II Therefore

2020

A PART APART APART   APART A PART APART
APART **A PART** A PART A PART APART APART
APART APART APART APART A PART APART
APART APART A PART A PART A PART APART
APART A PART A PART **APART APART APART**
A PART APART A PART A PART APART A PART
APART APART A PART A PART APART APART A
PART APART A PART **APART** APART A PART A
PART A PART APART A PART APART APART A
PART **A PART** A PART *A PART* APART APART
APART APART APART A PART APART APART
APART APART APART APART A PART A PART
APART APART **A PART** APART A PART APART
APART A PART APART   A PART **APART** APART

III THUS

For Maria de la Luz Valverde

On this Day of the Dead, you reach across shadows.
Such is the surprise light preaches across, shadows.

Do we wander fields, the white dunes, the river road?
No guide interprets, none teaches, across shadows.

The last minutes of day: sorrows drop, call us home.
Silences lengthening, like speech, across shadows.

Another Bridget

> *Upon receiving my grandmother's Irish passport,*
> *lost in an attic for fifty years.*

A *Free Stater*, her passport proclaims—someone else's politics
written in Irish. My grandmother fled for her own reasons.

Surely those are borrowed pearls she's wearing—shanty Irish, we.
No "special peculiarities" to declare; she's going,

and *sin é*. She'd sweep into New York beside a thousand
poor sisters, housemaids arrived and angering the locals

with their Catholicism, their Cork singsong. Journeying
for greener fields, they left everything, and the war.

At least she was legal. Paddys aren't Pedros, say
my old Irish aunts, fearing some storm from the south.

III Thus

Goodbye

Don't forget me
down the long way—
its amber of distance.

I am not slow light at mornings.
I am not a tree beside the road.
I am not whatever passes.

Curious once with breath
upon water, or within
some moment shaped

on rain, think again to say
I wandered well, soon gone
without my meanings done.

Moon and Planet—

so—so—I'd forgotten
long—my distance
through—this satined dark
—wistfulness at once
and I am lost —this beauty

now like painted light
within the mind—a moment's
face—if it should all drift
down—if it should all be gone
again against the earth

—to learn the wombword
of the night soon turning—
its persistent whispers
turning windward—song
that thrums with sky—

III T̲ʜᴜs

New York Winter, 49

I sensed on those streets the attenuated gestures

of workers; or, arm in arm, women talking,
moving along some thought that had left them
thirsting, worried, solicitous for the predictable

patterns of their days: moments at the corner bagel shop,
the bank's chiseled certainties. We've misplaced
ourselves, perhaps they think, then, thinking surer,

they light out for some pleasant past—symphonies, birds
at a window, sails white and fulling on the bay.
Down autumn's graying days, within this world

of dust and ash, what memory ever worth its weight?

III Thus

Caught Music

Aloft because chaos dances, elastic,
flowering. Generous, how impulse jumps—

kept lively. Melody nudges open—prospector,
questioning. Remember summer?

Tallying us, vireos, wings x-rayed yellow,
zeroed along bare cliffs. Drawn even from

graceless hollows—imagine—juncos, katydids,
luscious mango noons. Our passions

quickened. Rondos, serpentine: the unsung,
voiced with xylophones. Yodels. Zithers.

III Thus

Kepler's Last Autumn
> *Mensus eram coelos, nunc terrae metior umbras*
> *Mens coelestis erat, corporis umbra iacet.*

Imagine, I can't comprehend
what I see. It's all erosion and false-

shape of shadow—leaves me undone.
Explanations incomplete, journeys

abandoned midway over the mountains.
You expect the insight of sages, a silvered charm

that spirits us past chasms where
hollow takes hold. Know: trees stumble

through my nights same as yours. Oceans open.
Planets, memories, systems spin round

that moment we'll first know our minds.
If I promised, I've failed. If I loved you,

I regret. How we wander through loss,
following traces cut across the horizon.

III THUS

Part
     —for Tiberiu Rus

Always someone's leaving for good. Easy to
say. Open a window. Leave
a note beside the typewriter—who reads it

standing there wants a moment alone
to consider the current of
the words. What's done, is. Are there

apologies musty in an overcoat, creased into
a pocketbook? I imagine
hesitations over the phone. *I didn't want*

to go. I had to. Simple, like water runs cool
down this blue-green glass.
Always someone's on the way out. You?

III Thus

Goodwife's Prayer, Autumn 1653

Do I call after you, Lord, through the dark
hallways of leaves, this black forest,

in air so full and heavy it pulls against
one's journey? No motion in the trees.
Spirit voices from the far fields. I've heard

the cries of nightjars, seen them dive across
the last shadows of a day. The hills' faint,

failing outline—evenings I've seen it
whisper and go. I ask: have we come, too,
only to flicker and fade, only to seek you

now within the formless hollow of this
wilderness? Say. Speak. Let me know.

IV Regardless

Snow

Easy with sky, snow knows its fall.
Whitest within white. Acceptable to

winter because winter speaks through it.
Says, *taken upon the wind.* Says,

*shut up your houses. Night's falling,
too.* It whistles down the fields. Snow

won't stop, tasting chill, wraps around,
courses over. I think, *leave us ourselves*

*at least. These hours—I see how they spin
on the snow, spin and swim. . . until*

*we set out glad for the woods, abandon
paths, lean into the wind and let go.*

IV Regardless

Along Rockfall

At the heart of the canyon, along rockfall,
dry stream and limestone caves: the echoed call

of a hawk. A few live oaks grow here,
fed on the fractured light. Whisper-clear,
this flow of sun over sheer stones. Near
dry stream and limestone caves: the echoed call

that settles into the darknesses between
boulders. Even in the smallest crevice, green
growth. Lichen, extravagant as coral, and lean,
at the heart of the canyon, along rockfall,

shows itself, has its say where only we know.
Water wanders down rocks, spreads and slows
to a pattern that holds, builds, becomes below
dry stream and limestone caves: the echoed call

that reaches us as we strike camp unaware.
Breaks in the cliff face trace like tears
in living skin. We are anticipated everywhere. . .
at the heart of the canyon, along rockfall.

IV REGARDLESS

Blue Salvia in August

Making their soft assertions
of blue upon the walk, the last
salvia blooms fall. A mantis,

inch-long and brown, grazes
the bare seed-shafts—flagged
now in the fullness of summer.

Against each measured step, she stills,
head turned to learn how
the leaves harden against the heat.

IV Regardless

Climbing Rose

Bids us "think of spring before spring":
        this bud that blooms now, full
                and reaching, aimed toward opening.
Bids us think of spring before spring,
            trust motion, and flower. Something
            shapes, becomes, follows pull,
bids us think of spring. Before spring:
        this bud that blooms now, full.

IV REGARDLESS

Poets in Romania
 —*Cluj*

White. The sky is white. For the moment, I am
content, surprised to find I trust in detail.

I think of evenings, dark talk and *tuica*. Those
Romanian poets. What did they teach me? How little

one can say with certainty. That disintegration is
itself an evolution, a return—is finally the sere

white of distance. The rest: without definition,
utterly insignificant, absolute. And where will we be

until the end? Drinking toasts to the bittersweet
loss of the world. Drunken with wine and melody.

V Yet

Winter and Midnights

    Along the night, white

                       silences drift—a ghost-
glow from the streetlights.

Snow, left to the itself again,

    settles

                            now within
              sleep's broadening shadows.

www.ingramcontent.com/pod-product-compliance
Lightning Source LLC
Chambersburg PA
CBHW022123090426
42743CB00008B/972